1/10

Northern Lights

by Janet Piehl

Lerner Publications Company • Minneapolis

For Caitlin, Nicolai, and Amalia

Photo Acknowledgments

The images in this book are used with the permission of: © Photodisc/Getty Images, all backgrounds, p.15; © age fotostock/SuperStock, p. 4; © LOOK Die Bildagentur der Fotografen GmbH/Alamy, pp. 6, 10; © Iconica/Arctic-Images/Getty Images, pp. 7, 25; © iStockphoto.com/Roman Krochuk, pp. 8, 11, 16; © Ron Niebrugge/Alamy, p. 9; NASA-JPL, p. 12; © Koji Kitagawa/SuperStock, p. 14; © Gerald & Buff Corsi/Visuals Unlimited, p. 17; © Phil Degginger/Alamy, p. 18; © Taxi/World Perspectives/Getty Images, p. 20; © Doug Allan/The Image Bank/Getty Images, p. 21; © Astrofoto/Peter Arnold, Inc., p. 22; © All Canada Photos/Alamy, p. 24; © Aurora/Joel Sheagren/Getty Images, p. 26; © Stuart O'Sullivan/Stone/Getty Images, p. 27. Illustrations on pp.19, 28 by © Laura Westlund/Independent Picture Service.

Front cover: © Kevin Schafer/Photographer's Choice/Getty Images.
Back cover: © Photodisc/Getty Images.

Lerner Publications Company
A division of Lerner Publishing Group, Inc.
241 First Avenue North
Minneapolis, MN 55401

Website address: www.lernerbooks.com

Words in **bold type** are explained in a glossary on page 31.

Library of Congress Cataloging-in-Publication Data

Piehl, Janet.
    Northern lights / by Janet Piehl.
        p.   cm. — (Pull ahead books. Forces of nature)
    Includes index.
    ISBN 978-0-8225-8832-0 (lib. bdg. : alk. paper)
    1. Auroras—Juvenile literature. I. Title.
QC971.4.P54 2009
538'.768—dc22   2007038934

Manufactured in the United States of America
1 2 3 4 5 6 — BP — 14 13 12 11 10 09

Table of Contents

What Are the Northern Lights?...5

**What Causes the
  Northern Lights?** 13

**Where and When to See
  the Northern Lights** 23

**More about
  the Northern Lights**..............28

Northern Lights Facts 29

Further Reading 30

Glossary 31

Index 32

4

What Are the Northern Lights?

The northern night sky glows green. A cloud of bright light drifts across the sky. The light changes shape and color. Red rays flicker. What is happening?

The **northern lights** are out. The northern lights are a natural light show. They can be green, blue, yellow, red, pink, or purple.

The northern lights appear in different shapes.

Sometimes the northern lights look
curved.

Sometimes they look like curtains or clouds. Other times, they look like ribbons or rays.

The northern lights happen more than 60 miles (97 kilometers) above the ground.

They stretch thousands of miles across the northern sky.

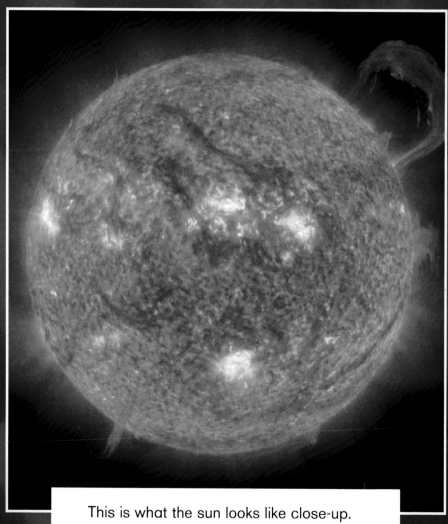

This is what the sun looks like close-up.

What Causes the Northern Lights?

The beginnings of the northern lights are at the sun. **Particles** stream out from the sun. The particles travel very fast through space. But Earth is far away from the sun. The particles take two or three days to reach Earth.

Earth's atmosphere as seen from space

The particles enter Earth's **atmosphere**. The atmosphere is a layer of **gases**. It surrounds Earth.

14

The particles meet the gases in the atmosphere. They give off light when they meet. The lights are called **auroras**.

Auroras forming in Earth's atmosphere

Auroras in the northern sky are called northern lights.

Auroras over the northern state of Alaska

But why are the lights in the northern sky?

Imagine that Earth is a **magnet**. A magnet pulls certain metal objects toward it. Earth also pulls objects toward it.

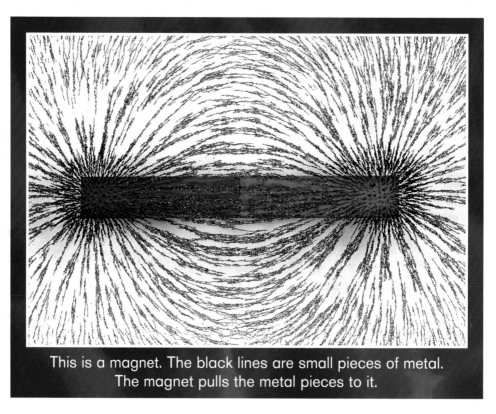

This is a magnet. The black lines are small pieces of metal. The magnet pulls the metal pieces to it.

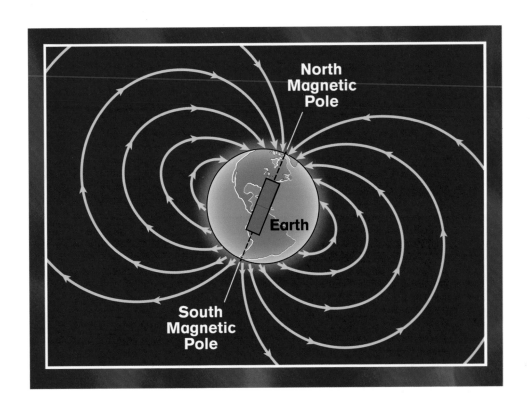

Earth's **magnetic pull** is strongest near the North Pole and the South Pole. Particles from the sun are pulled toward the poles.

Northern lights over the North Pole as seen from space

The particles react with Earth's atmosphere. Auroras form near Earth's poles. The northern lights are auroras near the North Pole.

Auroras near the South Pole are called **southern lights**.

Southern lights over the continent of Antarctica

Northern lights glow above a town in Norway.

Where and When to See the Northern Lights

People in countries like Canada, Norway, Sweden, Finland, and Russia often see the northern lights. Sometimes people see them in the northern United States. People in Alaska see them often.

Northern lights in spring over Canada

The best months to see the northern lights are September, October, March, and April.

Northern lights are present during the day. But you can only see them at night. Then the sky is dark enough.

The northern lights are best seen around midnight.

What do you see in the northern night sky?

MORE ABOUT THE NORTHERN LIGHTS

This map shows where the northern lights can be seen in North America, the Arctic, and Europe.

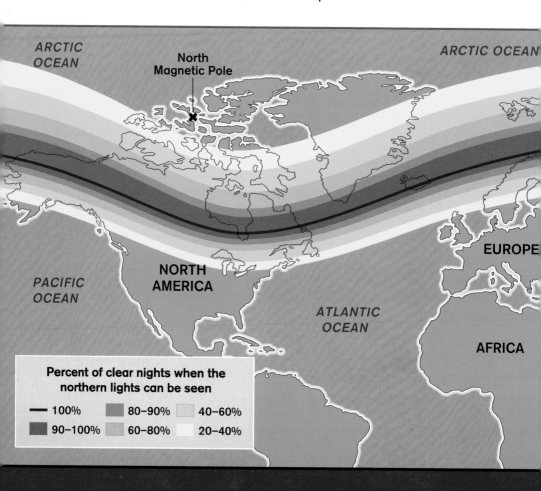

ARCTIC OCEAN

North Magnetic Pole

ARCTIC OCEAN

PACIFIC OCEAN

NORTH AMERICA

ATLANTIC OCEAN

EUROPE

AFRICA

Percent of clear nights when the northern lights can be seen

- —— 100%
- 90–100%
- 80–90%
- 60–80%
- 40–60%
- 20–40%

Northern Lights Facts

- Another way to say "northern lights" is "aurora borealis." That is Latin for "northern dawn." Another way to say "southern lights" is "aurora australis." That means "southern dawn."

- Many people say they hear sounds when they see the northern lights. But scientists have not been able to prove that the sounds are real.

- Northern peoples have told many stories to explain the northern lights. People in Finland thought a fox running through the mountains made the northern lights. Some Native American groups thought the northern lights were fires burning in the sky.

- A Norwegian scientist named Kristian Birkeland made many important discoveries about the northern lights in the early 1900s. His work helped scientists to understand the northern lights.

Further Reading

Books

Mitchell, Melanie. *Earth*. Minneapolis: Lerner Publications Company, 2004.

Mitchell, Melanie. *Sun*. Minneapolis: Lerner Publications Company, 2004.

Walker, Sally. *Magnetism*. Minneapolis: Lerner Publications Company, 2006.

Websites

Auroras: Paintings in the Sky
http://www.exploratorium.edu/learning_studio/auroras/index.html
Find photos and answers to questions about auroras on this site.

NORDLYS-Northern Lights
http://www.northern-lights.no/
This Norwegian site gives information about the northern lights. It also has northern lights paintings and stories.

Virtual Finland: Aurora Borealis
http://www.virtual.finland.fi/Nature_Environment/aurora/index.html
This site has videos of the northern lights and tells how the northern lights form.

Glossary

atmosphere: the layer of gases that surrounds Earth

auroras: a special kind of light that can sometimes be seen in the night sky. Auroras appear most often near Earth's poles.

gases: substances, such as air, that can change size or shape

magnet: an object that pulls certain metal objects toward it. Magnets are often made of metal themselves.

magnetic pull: a magnet's power to bring objects toward it

northern lights: the glow in the sky that appears close to the North Pole

particles: tiny pieces

southern lights: the glow in the sky that appears close to the South Pole

Index

atmosphere, 14, 15, 20

auroras, 15, 16, 20, 21, 29

colors of northern lights, 5, 6

Earth's poles, 19–21

magnetic pull, 18, 19

shapes of northern lights, 5, 7–9

southern lights, 21, 29

sun particles, 13–15, 19, 20

when to see northern lights, 24–26

where to see northern lights, 10, 11, 23, 28